FOCUS

on Writing

D0731090

Writing

Book 3

**John Jackman and
Wendy Wren**

Collins

FOCUS

on Writing

Using this book

This book will help you to develop your writing skills to become a really successful writer.

What's in a unit

Each unit is set out in the same way as the example here.

Unit heading

This tells you what you will be learning about

Think about it

Activities to practise, check and develop your writing skills

The text

The texts have been carefully selected to demonstrate all major genre types, from fiction to non-fiction. Annotations point out useful techniques and help you to see what really works

Now try these

Activities to stretch and extend your writing skills

UNIT 15 — Using information

When researching facts for a report, keep a note of where you found the information. Then make sure you tell your readers which books you have used.

Magnets: from rocks to computers

Source of definition

The word 'magnet', according to *The Concise Oxford Dictionary*, comes from the Greek word 'magnesetos', which means stone of Magnesia.

Writer of the book where information was found

Most of us assume magnets are made in factories. They are now, but the original magnets were certainly not made in a factory or bought from a shop. As Nigel Bennett explains:

'The magnet has a very long history and can be traced back to a part of the country of Greece called Thessaly. Many thousands of years ago, in a district called Magnesia, people discovered a rock which seemed to do strange things.

'The rock, called magnetite, was found to attract anything made of iron. It also had other properties. It was later found to rotate in a certain direction and point north or south.'

It is surprising how much we use magnets in modern technology. Magnets are found in everything from video cassettes to computers. In his book, *Electricity and Magnetism*, Dr Brian Knapp tells us that:

Title and author of another source of information

'Magnets don't have to look like bars. Some of the most useful are shaped into tapes and disks.

'A cassette tape is a long plastic ribbon, coated with minute iron particles (look for the non-shiny side). As the tape moves

it goes past a tiny electromagnet called a recording head. Electric signals reaching the recording head set up patterns of magnetism on the tape.

'Computers store information on disks that look something like a record. The disk, often called a floppy disk because it is made of bendy plastic, has an iron coating on its surface.

'The computer "reads" from and "writes" onto the disk using a small head just like the tape recorder. The disk shown here has 800 000 pieces of information stored on it in magnetic form. The biggest disks can store many millions of pieces of information.'

More details of the books mentioned

Bibliography

1 Bennett, Nigel, *Magnets, Batteries and Globes*, Macmillan
2 Knapp, Brian, *Electricity and Magnetism*, Atlantic Europe Publishing Company

Think about it

Write a sentence to answer each of these questions.
a) Who wrote about the history of magnets in his book?
b) What was the book called?
c) Who published the book?
d) Which dictionary is quoted in the passage?
e) Write the names of two other dictionaries.
f) Whose book tells about the use of magnets in computers?
g) What was the book called?
h) Who published the book?
i) What other sort of book could you refer to for information about magnets?
j) Make a list of the author, title and publisher of three other books in which you can find useful information on magnets and magnetism.

Now try these

1. Write a few paragraphs about other uses of magnets or write about the discovery and uses of electricity. Use the books in your school library or from home. Don't forget to use quotations from the authors of the books you use (put these inside speech marks), and write the details of their books in a bibliography at the end of your work.
2. Choose a subject that you are learning about at the moment. Make a list of books in your library in which you might find information about the subject. Make a bibliography. Use the surnames of the authors and list the books in alphabetical order by authors' names.

46

47

Contents

Looking at book covers

Book covers and book blurbs help us to predict what a book is about. Here is the front cover of *Redwall* by Brian Jacques.

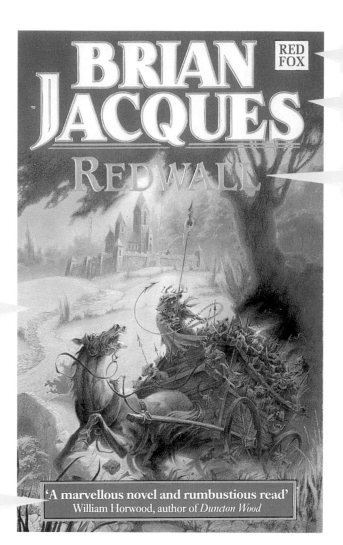

Publisher's logo

Author

Title

Cover illustration

Comment by another author

'A marvellous novel and rumbustious read'
William Horwood, author of *Duncton Wood*

Think about it

1. Write short answers for these questions.
   a) Who is the author of the book?
   b) Who published the book?
   c) What is the title of the book?
   d) What does William Horwood think about the book?
   e) Look at the cover illustration. What do you think the book is about?

Here is the back cover of *Redwall*. The information on the back cover is a 'blurb'.

Summary of the opening

It is the start of the Summer of the Late Rose. Redwall Abbey, the peaceful home of a community of mice, slumbers in the warmth of a summer afternoon. The mice are busy preparing for a great Jubilee feast.

But not for long. Cluny is coming! The evil one-eyed rat warlord is advancing with his battle-scarred mob. And Cluny wants Redwall ...

Recommended reading age

Nominated for a prize

Redwall is an extraordinarily powerful first novel and should be read by everyone over the age of nine. Written by an ex-Liverpool docker, it was nominated for the Carnegie Award and has now sold nearly one million copies worldwide.

Information about the author

Comment from a magazine

'Compulsive'
British Book News

Number of copies sold

REDWALL is also available on audio tape, read by Brian Jacques, from Random House Tellastory

Information about the book on tape

ISBN number

ISBN 0-09-951200-9

9 780099 512004

Price

UK £4.99 CAN $7.95

2. Answer these questions in sentences.
   a) Why do you think the summary of the book stops at 'And Cluny wants Redwall...'?
   b) How can you tell that the book is already very popular?
   c) How do you know that Brian Jacques has never written a novel before?
   d) Why is there a comment from another author on the front cover and from a magazine on the back cover?
   e) By using the information on the front and back covers, explain why you would or would not like to read this book.

Here is the back cover of a novel called *Flour Babies* by Anne Fine.
Look carefully at the information on the cover and answer the questions.

Let it be flour babies.
Let chaos reign.

When the annual school science fair comes round, Mr Cartright's class don't get to work on the Soap Factory, the Maggot Farm or the Exploding Custard Tins. To their intense disgust they get the Flour Babies – sweet little six-pound bags of flour that must be cared for at all times.

Young Simon Martin, a committed hooligan, approaches the task with little enthusiasm. But, as the days pass, he not only grows fond of his flour baby, he also comes to learn more than he ever could have imagined about the pressures and strains of being a parent.

CHOSEN BY CHILDREN AS THE PICK OF THE YEAR FOR THE FEDERATION OF CHILDREN'S BOOK GROUPS

'Funny and moving, *Flour Babies* is an uplifting, self-raising story' – *Guardian*

Cover illustration by Derek Brazell

PUFFIN

U.K. £4.99
AUST. $9.95
(recommended)
CAN. $6.99

ISBN 0-14-036147-2

91401

9 780140 361476

3. a) What is the event the story is based around?
   b) What do the children have to do with the flour babies?
   c) What does Simon Martin think about looking after the flour babies?
   d) What does looking after the flour babies help to teach the children?
   e) What information shows the book is popular with children?
   f) Why is the quote from the *Guardian* on the back cover?
   g) Who has published the book?
   h) Does the blurb make you want to read the book?

Now try these

1. Look back at the front cover of *Redwall* to remind you of the information that goes on to the front cover of a book.
   Draw a front cover for *Flour Babies*.
2. Two children have an adventure which starts in a deserted house and includes a hair-raising journey, a wizard and a treasure hunt.
   Design the front and back covers for this book.

Continuing a story

This is the beginning of a book called *Goodnight Mister Tom* in which the writer introduces us to two of the main characters, Thomas Oakley and William Beech.

Not very polite

'Yes,' said Tom bluntly, on opening the front door. 'What d'you want?'

A harassed middle-aged woman in a green coat and felt hat stood on his step. He glanced at the armband on her sleeve. She gave an awkward smile.

'I'm the Billeting Officer for this area,' she began.

Tom makes the woman feel uncomfortable

'Oh yes, and what's that got to do wi' me?'

She flushed slightly. 'Well, Mr, Mr...'

'Oakley. Thomas Oakley.'

'Ah, thank you, Mr Oakley.' She paused and took a deep breath. 'Mr Oakley, with the declaration of war imminent...'

Notice how Tom speaks

Tom waved his hand. 'I know all that. Git to the point. What d'you want?' He noticed a small boy at her side.

'It's him I've come about,' she said. 'I'm on my way to your village hall with the others.'

'What others?'

She stepped to one side. Behind the large iron gate which stood at the end of the graveyard were a small group of

Detailed description

children. Many of them were filthy and very poorly clad. Only a handful had a blazer or a coat. They all looked bewildered and exhausted. One tiny dark-haired girl in the front was hanging firmly on to a new teddy-bear.

The woman touched the boy at her side and pushed him forward.

'There's no need to tell me,' said Tom. 'It's obligatory and it's for the war effort.'

'You are entitled to choose your child, I know,' began the woman apologetically.

Shows he isn't interested

Tom gave a snort.

'But,' she continued, 'his mother wants him to be with someone who's religious or near a church. She was quite adamant. Said she would only let him be evacuated if he was.'

'Was what?' asked Tom impatiently.

'Near a church.'

Detailed description

Tom took a second look at the child. The boy was thin and sickly-looking, pale with limp sandy hair and dull grey eyes.

'His name's Willie,' said the woman.

Notice Willie's silence

Willie, who had been staring at the ground, looked up. Round his neck, hanging from a piece of string, was a cardboard label. It read 'William Beech'.

Detailed description

Tom was well into his sixties, a healthy, robust, stockily-built man with a head of thick white hair. Although he was of average height, in Willie's eyes he was a towering giant with skin like coarse, wrinkled brown paper and a voice like thunder.

Willie's viewpoint

He glared at Willie. 'You'd best come in,' he said abruptly.

from _Goodnight Mister Tom_ by Michelle Magorian

Think about it

1. The style of an author is the way he or she writes.
   Look at this list and copy the words that you think describe this author's style.
   a) funny
   b) serious
   c) uses description
   d) uses dialogue
   e) uses fantasy
   f) creates real-life situations
2. What sort of character do you think Tom Oakley is? Write your impressions from the text.
3. What do you think Willie is thinking and feeling while Tom and the woman are talking?
4. How does the writer make you feel about Willie?

Now try these

1. The extract stops where Willie is invited into Tom's house. Write the next part of the story as you think the author might have written it.
   – What happens?
   – What do Tom and Willie say to each other?
   – How does Willie react to being left with Tom?
2. While Willie lives with Tom Oakley, he has to go to the village school and he is put in a class with younger children because he cannot read or write.
   Write the part of the story about Willie's first day at school as you think the author might have written it. You will have to introduce some new characters, such as the teacher and other pupils. You will also have to describe what happens and how Willie feels about the experience.

Similes and metaphors

A simile compares two things by saying one thing is like the other.
Similes use 'as' and 'like' to make the comparison.

> Simile comparing the bus and the butterfly

Symphony in Yellow

An omnibus across the bridge
Crawls like a yellow butterfly,
And here and there, a passer-by
Shows like a little restless midge.

> Simile comparing a person with an insect

> Simile comparing the fog to a scarf

Big barges full of yellow hay
Are moored against the shadowy wharf
And, like a yellow silken scarf,
The thick fog hangs along the quay.

The yellow leaves begin to fade
And flutter from the Temple elms,
And at my feet the pale green Thames
Lies like a rod of rippled jade.

Oscar Wilde

> Simile comparing the river with jade (a type of green stone)

A metaphor compares two things without using 'as' or 'like'. Metaphors are sometimes hard to spot. They make the comparison by saying one thing actually is the other.

The Toaster

A silver-scaled Dragon with jaws flaming red
Sits at my elbow and toasts my bread.
I hand him fat slices, and then one by one,
He hands them back when he sees they are done.

> Metaphor that says the toaster is a dragon

Steam Shovel

> Metaphor that says the steam shovel is a dinosaur

The dinosaurs are not all dead.
I saw one raise its iron head
To watch me walking down the road
Beyond our house today.
Its jaws were dripping with a load
Of earth and grass that it had cropped.
It must have heard me where I stopped,
Snorted white steam my way,
And stretched its long neck out to see,
And chewed, and grinned quite amiably.

Charles Malam

Think about it

1. Two things can be compared to each other because something about them is similar.
   What do you think is similar about:
   a) the bus and the butterfly?
   b) the person and an insect?
   c) the fog and a scarf?
   d) the river and jade?
2. Make up some similes to compare these pairs of things.
   a) a rose and a sunset
   b) someone's legs and a stick insect
   c) someone's hair and a raven
   d) someone running and a cheetah
3. In your own words, write why you think the poet says the toaster is a dragon.
4. In your own words, write why you think the poet says the steam shovel is a dinosaur.

5. Change the comparisons in these sentences from a simile to a metaphor. The first one has been done to help you.

   a) The water was as flat and shiny as a mirror.

   The water was a flat, shiny mirror.

   b) The moon was like a shining lamp.

   c) The kitten was like a fluffy ball.

Now try these

1. a) Choose your favourite simile from the poem 'Symphony in Yellow' and say why you like it.

   b) Which metaphor do you like better, 'The Toaster' **or** 'Steam Shovel'? Say why.

2. Write a metaphor to describe each of the following as if it were an animal. The first one has been done to help you.

   a) a wave

   The wave is a dog at play.

   b) a garden hose

   c) a hairbrush

   d) a flag pole

3. Try writing your own poem using similes and metaphors.
   Begin by choosing an object and make notes about what each part of that object looks like, feels like and sounds like.
   Use your notes to write similes and metaphors about the object.
   Use your similes and metaphors in your poem.

Stage directions

Stage directions are included in a playscript to give instructions to the performers.

The Long Hike

Scene 1: In a wood towards dusk.

Telling which side of the stage to enter

John and Harry enter stage left. Harry is walking briskly but John is dragging his feet and looking tired.

John: *(flopping down on the ground)* I'm tired.

Telling how to move

Harry: *(looking at the map)* Come on, John. It can't be far now.

John: *(crossly)* That's what you said half an hour ago!

Harry: *(sitting down next to John)* OK. We'll rest here for a few minutes, but we can't stay long. It will be dark soon.

Telling how to speak

John: *(sounding worried)* What will we do if we don't get there before dark?

Harry: *(jumping up quickly)* We won't get anywhere if we stay here.

Telling what to do

John: *(getting up slowly)* All right, I'm coming, but this is the last time I go hiking with the scouts!

Telling which side of the stage to exit

Harry marches off briskly stage right with John following slowly behind and grumbling to himself.

Here is the next scene of the play.

Scene 2

Harry: I'm not sure where we are.

John: That's great. Now you have got us lost!

Harry: I've got us lost? We are both supposed to be reading this map. You've left it all to me.

John: Well, it's no good having an argument about it. That's not going to get us out of this wood.

Harry: Yes, you're right. Let's sit down, look at the map and see if we can find out where we are.

John: We started from there and followed that path and we should be there.

Harry: I know what we've done! Look! We've taken the wrong path back there by the stream.

John: What was that?

Harry: What?

John: That noise.

Harry: Look! Look at that strange light coming through the trees!

John: I think we had better get out of here!

Think about it

1. Look at the stage direction for John when he says 'That's what you said half an hour ago'.
   a) What does it tell the actor about the way to act?
   b) If the actor is supposed to be feeling very happy about the hike, what stage direction could you write instead of 'crossly'?

2. Look at the stage direction for John when he says 'What will we do if we don't get there before dark?'
   a) How does the actor need to say these words?
   b) If the actor was not at all concerned about it getting dark, what stage direction could you write instead of 'sounding worried'?

3. The stage direction tells Harry what to do when he says 'Come on, John. It can't be far now'. He has to look at the map. Write a stage direction which tells the actor how to say this line.

4. Scene 2 of the playscript has no details about the setting. Write where the scene is set and what it looks like.
5. Scene 2 has no stage directions. Read it through carefully and decide:
   a) how the lines should be said
   b) where an actor needs to know what to do
   c) where an actor needs to know how to move
   d) which side of the stage an actor enters and exits from.
   Think about the stage directions that might be necessary and copy out the playscript with your stage directions in place.

Now try this

Choose one of the following play titles and write the opening scene:
a) The Picnic
b) The Birthday Party
c) Sports Day
Plan and write the scene in this order:
a) Characters
   How many characters are there in this scene?
   What are their names?
   What sort of people are they?
b) Setting
   Where is the scene set?
   What will the stage look like?
c) Script
   What is the dialogue (conversation) going to be about?
   Write the first draft of the dialogue.
d) Stage directions
   What stage directions will you need to add?
   You can use stage directions to show:
   – how an actor moves
   – how an actor speaks
   – what an actor has to do
   – which side of the stage an actor enters and exits from.
e) Make a neat copy of your scene, setting it out like Scene 1 of *The Long Hike*.

Costumes, props and sets

If you were going to put on the play *The Long Hike*, there are many other things you need to consider apart from the script.

1 Costumes

You need detailed drawings of how the actors are to be dressed.

Purple scarf

Green shirt

Lots of badges

Black trousers

Strong hiking boots

Scarf badly tied

Sleeves rolled up

Few badges

Trainers

Harry   John

2 Props

This is an abbreviation for 'properties' which are the objects actors carry or use on stage.

Harry's rucksack

John's rucksack

3 Sets

The sets, or what the stage looks like, are very important for the audience. There might be different sets in one play. You need detailed drawings of each set.

Scene 1: In a wood towards dusk.

Thick background of trees

Evening sunlight through trees

A definite path

A clearing

Scene 2: In a different part of the wood.

Trees now take up more of the stage

Dark

A few boulders about

A less definite path

Think about it

1. What are the differences between the way Harry and John are dressed? What does it tell you about them?
2. Look at the two rucksacks.
   Which is more suitable for a long hike?
   What does this tell you about the characters?
3. Why do you think costumes are important?
4. How would the audience know that Scene 2 is in a different part of the wood?
5. Why is it important that they realise this?

Now try this

Look at the playscript and stage directions which you wrote for unit 4.
You need to make drawings and label them.
Plan and write your work in this order.

a) Costumes
   Decide what each of your characters will wear on stage.
   Remember that how characters are dressed often gives the audience a clue as to what sort of person they are.
   Draw and label a costume for each character.

b) Props
   Think carefully about the objects an actor has to carry or use on stage.
   Draw and label each prop, making sure to include the name of the character who needs it.

c) Set
   You need to imagine clearly what the stage will look like for your scene.
   Draw and label the set, remembering to include details about the time of day and where objects are placed on the stage.

Writing reports

We often need to write reports about events to tell other people what has happened. The way we write depends on who will be reading our report, our audience. Here is the same event reported in two different ways.

WALLINGTON WALLOP THE WANDERERS

Jim Waller,
Sports Correspondent

Saturday's match was a cracker! Wallington Town Boys had fought hard to reach the final of the Nuffield Soccer Shield after a long, hard season, and from the kick-off at the town stadium, it was clear they were not going to be over-awed, either by the venue or the opposition from Shellingford Wanderers. It was a credit to both teams that so many people had turned out on this bitterly cold day.

Shellingford won the toss, and 10 year-old James Roberts was soon showing why. Even though he is the youngest in the Wanderers team, he is the player everyone has been talking about this season. For pace and skill, he had no match. Brian Hanson, the coach, put two defenders to closely mark Roberts, and for the first 20 minutes this was very effective. But then the inevitable happened. Young Alex Humphries slipped on the frosty surface, and that was all Roberts needed to weave past the other defender and strike a 20 metre drive hard and high into the back of Wallington's net.

Was this the beginning of the end? Would Wallington crack under the pressure of a powerful Shellingford now that their tails were up? If that was on the spectators' minds, it certainly wasn't in the minds of our lads. Matt Jackson, who recently came to the town and who has made such a difference to our mid-field this season, was out to show Shellingford they weren't getting the cup without a fight. Inside three minutes a long run and a beautifully judged pass to Ben Lupton, Town's super new striker, was all that was needed to put our boys back on even terms.

The second half was an end-to-end battle. Tension sometimes showed, with some unnecessary loss of possession, but neither side could make it count, and ***continued on next page***

Introduction to set the scene

Events in order, but with added comment

on the final whistle the score was 1-1.

It is a great pity that such an exciting match, and such an important one, should be decided on penalties. Some of the players found it tough to watch — but not as tough as some of the supporters! Our new goalkeeper Ashok Kulkarni came up trumps, and when everything depended on the last penalty he kept his cool. Little wonder his team carried him off the field shoulder high!

Closing statement

Let's hope next season our lads can do us as proud again, and carry off not just the cup, but the league title as well.

6 Ashmore Drive
Wallington
Midshire
WA4 7TG

27th April

Dear Manjit

I hope you are getting on well at your new school. We are missing not having you in our team, but I thought you'd like to know how the game went on Saturday. You know where we were playing, which was a bit scary, but fun. There were hundreds of people watching!

Friendly opening giving reason for writing

Shellingford had a really good team, and a brilliant new striker, but Mr Hanson put Lee and Alex on to marking him. That was fine until Alex slipped over and their striker shot so hard I couldn't get near it! I thought we were in real trouble then, but our defence didn't panic and Matt Jackson (a new boy who's only just joined the team) put Ben through to score a real beauty!

Main part of letter, telling Manjit what he'd be most interested to know

That was the final score, so it was a penalty shoot-out. It was then I was wishing you hadn't moved and were still the goalie. I saved the first four shots, only just. Their goalie saved the first three, but then let one in. That meant I needed to save the last one, and we'd win the cup. And I did! That was the most terrific feeling in the world. You should have heard the cheers. Everyone went mad. They all said I was a hero, but really I was a bit lucky, because the ball came straight at me!

Get your Mum and Dad to bring you to see us play next season. Then we can show you the cup!

Conclusion

Your friend,
Ashok

20

Think about it

1. Write short answers for these questions.
   a) Who wrote the report for the newspaper?
   b) Who was his audience?
   c) Did he know them all?
   d) Who wrote the letter?
   e) Who was his audience?
   f) Did he know him?

2. Answer these questions with sentences.
   a) Which report gives the most information about where the match took place? Why?
   b) How can we tell that this report appeared in the local Wallington paper, and not the Shellingford paper?
   c) Why didn't Ashok even bother to tell Manjit where the game was being played, or that it was the cup final?
   d) What is Ashok's letter mostly about? Why does he think this will interest Manjit?

Now try these

1. Write a report for your school magazine about a visit your class has made. Don't forget to:
   a) set the scene, saying where you went, and when
   b) write an interesting account of the main events, in the correct order
   c) finish with a thoughtful final paragraph, saying whether it was a good trip, if you enjoyed it, and perhaps whether or not you would like to go again
   d) think of a catchy headline.

2. Imagine that you had a best friend who left the school just a few days before the trip. Write a letter to your friend about the trip, telling of the things he or she would be most interested to read about.

Different sorts of records

Personal diaries record facts, but the details are less important than the writer's thoughts and opinions. In contrast, in some reports, like police reports, the facts are most important and they must be accurate.

Date of events being recorded

23rd September

Facts and feelings about the day – lots to record

It has been a bad day. First I was late for school because Mum made me clean my shoes. Then Ginnie and I had an argument. Worst of all (because Ginnie and I are really best friends and we will make up tomorrow) was when I got home from school. The shed door was open and my bike was nowhere to be seen. A burglar had broken into our shed and stolen it! I cried a bit, but when I phoned Mum, she said not to worry. She said she would come home early and she would phone the police. She also said that if they couldn't find my bike, she thought it would be covered on the insurance, so I should be able to get another one.

Dad was really mad when he saw what had happened to his padlock.

When Mum came home we called the police station, and they said they would send PC Brown to our house tomorrow, which is good because it's a Saturday.

I do hope I get my bike back. It was the best bike I've ever had, and I was just getting really good at riding it. I wish people wouldn't steal things!

Date of events being recorded

24th September

PC Brown came today. I told him all about it and I felt a little better. I hope he can find my bike.

Facts and feelings about the day – less to record than yesterday

MIDSHIRE COUNTY CONSTABULARY

Reporting Officer: *PC Brown*

Date of incident: *23rd September*

Time of incident: *Between 1 p.m. and 3.45 p.m.*

Date reported: *23rd September*

Person who reported: *Mrs Sabina Smith*

Date statement taken: *24th September*

Address/location of incident: *26 Kelvedon Road, Bramsdon Midshire*

Statement of witness: *Mandy Smith, owner of bike*

When I arrived home from school, I saw that our shed door was open. I went to close it so that it wouldn't blow and break the hinges. It was then that I noticed that my bike had gone. I looked behind the shed and in the garage, as I sometimes leave it in those places. It was nowhere to be seen. I also saw that the padlock on the shed door had been broken, and realised that someone must have stolen my bike. Mum said the shed was closed when she left for work at one o'clock.

Details of goods stolen/damaged: *Wentworth Mountain Bike; nearly new (about 2 months old); red with gold paint; left-hand grip slightly damaged; padlock on shed broken*

Value of goods stolen: *Approximately £185*

Location diagram:

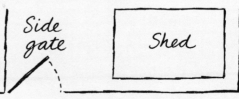

Signed: *Mandy Smith*   Date: *24th September*

Think about it

1. Write short answers for these questions.
   a) Who wrote the diary entry?
   b) Who was her audience?
   c) Who wrote the police report?
   d) Why was it written?
   e) Which report of the lost bike contained more facts?
   f) Which report contained more thoughts and feelings?
2. Make a list of the most important facts in the police report.
3. Why was Mandy so upset that her bike had been stolen?

Now try these

1. One day, as you were on your way to school, you saw a lorry skid on the ice and run into a lamppost. A police officer asks you to prepare a statement. Write it out like the one PC Brown wrote when Mandy reported her stolen bike. You may need to draw a diagram to show a plan of the road, and where the lorry skidded. Remember, it is only the facts that you should write, not how you felt when the accident happened.
2. Write an entry about seeing the lorry skid for your diary.
   Tell what happened, how you felt, and what you did.

Writing instructions

Good instructions are clear and easy to follow.
Tara and Jonathon made a kite. Each one wrote instructions on how to do this.
Tara did hers on a word processor.

Jonathon's instructions

Mrs Lindsay had been teaching us about kites. She told us that they were invented in China more than 2300 years ago. When our teacher asked us to design a kite that could fly, this is what we did.

First we collected the materials that we thought we needed. Tara brought a big plastic bag to school and I managed to persuade my dad to let me have some masking tape that was left over from when we had been respraying the rusty patch on the car. I also found some bamboo canes in the garden shed, which I thought would be good for the struts. But neither Tara nor I had any string at home, so we will get some with our pocket money on the way home tonight.

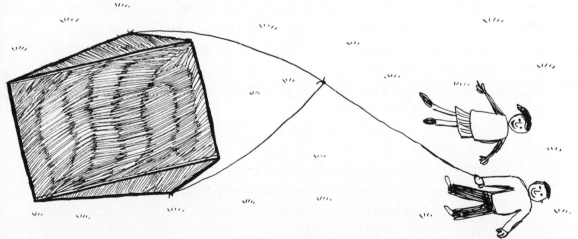

In my picture you can see the shape. You need to cut this from the sheet of plastic. Fix the two bamboo canes from top to bottom. Tie a loop of string from one bamboo cane to the other, passing through the holes in the plastic.

Tara's instructions

Object of the instructions

This is how to make a kite with six sides.

Equipment and materials needed:

List of equipment and materials

- one large plastic bin liner
- 2 thin sticks (thin bamboo canes work well)
- masking tape
- a ball of string
- scissors

Here is a diagram of the kite.

Detailed diagram often helps

About ¼ length of kite

thin wood

bridle point

tape over hole

dustbin liner

About ¾ length of kite

bridle (about 400 cm)

masking tape

attach line here

Clear and concise instructions, with a warning about any risks

Instructions

1. Cut the plastic to the correct shape, with the widest part about a quarter down from the top of the kite. The shape is important but the actual length is not. You can adjust the measurements according to the size of the plastic and the length of the sticks you have.
2. With the masking tape, fix the sticks firmly at the top and bottom of the plastic.
3. Fix each stick to the plastic sheet in three or four other places.
4. Make four small holes as show in the diagram.
5. Attach the bridle carefully and firmly as shown. (The bridle is the string going round the back of the kite from which the control line is attached.)
6. Attach the string in the centre of the bridle.

Whenever flying kites you must keep clear of overhead power lines!

Think about it

1. If you were going to make a kite, which of the two sets of instructions do you think would be easier to follow? Why?
2. Why is Tara's diagram more useful than Jonathon's picture?
3. Think of something that you have made recently. Write detailed instructions so that someone else could use them to make it.
4. Think of something you do on your computer. It might be loading software or playing a game. Write detailed instructions for doing this. Your audience is anyone who has never used your computer.

Now try these

1. Look at this diagram. It shows how to make a model of Concorde Mach 2 from thin card, but the instructions have been lost. Write the instructions that should go with the diagram.
   Start with a list of materials and equipment needed.
   Make the instructions clear and simple.

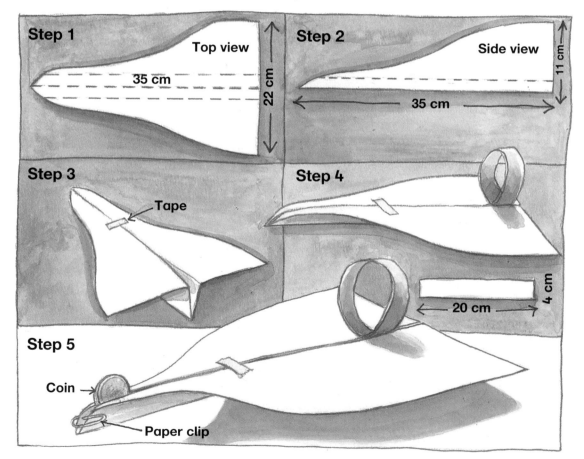

2. Follow Tara's instructions and make a kite like the one she and Jonathon made.

Notes for a talk, and using abbreviations

When we give a talk, we need to make notes about what we want to tell our listening audience.

This is how you might give a talk about rocks.

First, collect your information

1 Here are some pages from an information book. Can you find other books about rocks?

> There is a saying, 'as hard as a rock'. We think of rocks as being hard, tough and strong. Our Earth is made of rocks, many different sorts, but they are not all hard, and even if they are now, they haven't always been. If you walk along a beach, you will often see many different coloured rocks. Even grains of sand are tiny pieces of rock, and mud and clay are very soft rocks.

> Millions of years ago, our Earth was a ball of molten rock. As it slowly cooled, hard rocks formed on the surface, like a skin on thick custard. These rocks are called the 'crust' of the Earth. But deep down inside, the rocks are still extremely hot, so hot that they are still runny like thick, very, very hot custard. Sometimes, when there is an earthquake and the crust cracks, some of these molten rocks force their way to the surface. This molten rock is called lava, and often forms a volcano on the surface of the Earth.

Over thousands of years, the sea and rivers tumble and roll rocks about. The rocks break up and small pieces get chipped off. These pieces get smaller and smaller and

eventually become sand or mud. Finally the sand and mud settles to the bottom of the sea or river beds in layers, rather like a huge liquorice allsort. Sometimes a volcanic eruption may spread a layer of lava on the sand or mud as well, making a different layer. Then, perhaps millions of years later, the land rises or the sea drains away, and the sand and mud and volcanic layers can be seen as layers of rocks.

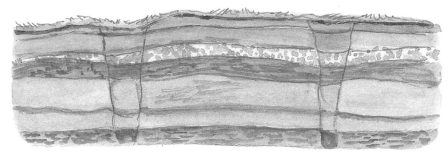

Even though we can't usually notice it, the Earth's crust is moving slowly all the time, and the layers get bent and buckled. If you look at the side of a cliff or a road embankment you can sometimes see all the different bands of rock, just like a bent liquorice allsort!

Make your notes

2 Next, skim through the information books and encyclopedia entries. Look for the key words and phrases and make notes of the main points and other things that interest you. Don't forget to include the information you already know in your notes.

Abbreviations are quicker

The notes are for you, so you can use short forms called abbreviations. You can invent your own abbreviations, but here are some ideas to get you started:

& = and   **inc.** = including   **∵** = because   **∴** = therefore

gd = good   **e.g.** = for example   **i.e.** = that is   **etc.** = and so on

Plan your talk

3 What are the main things you will tell your audience? Work out the best order for the information. It could be:
a) rocks are all different
b) how the Earth's crust was formed
c) why rocks are found in layers
d) what we use rocks for today.

Collect examples to show

4 Collect and make things to show your audience. These could include:
- different types of rock from your area (Don't forget some sand and clay as well as lumps of rock.)
- big, clear diagrams to help you explain some parts of your talk
- examples of rocks used in everyday life such as bricks and pottery (made from clay), coal for heating, granite chips for roads, glass (made from sand).

Prepare brief notes

5 Make notes of what you will say. Write on a piece of card a few words to jog your memory, not every word you want to say. Do it like this:

Rocks are all different
imagine a beach
boulders, sand, mud — all rocks
some hard, some soft

Interesting start

How the Earth's crust was formed
show diagram of Earth's crust
molten lava, like custard

Why rocks are found in layers
sea / rivers make sand / mud / clay
layers form, liquorice allsort
sometimes volcano lava
sometimes land rises or sea falls
land gets bent (diagram)

What we use rocks for today
show examples / talk about them

Close

Think about it

1. What is an abbreviation?
2. Write these words and phrases.
   Next to each write a possible abbreviation.
   a) because   b) and so on   c) and   d) for example
   e) volcano   f) important   g) especially   h) therefore
3. Make a list of the main stages you would go through to give a talk to your class.

Now try these

Collect the information for a talk on a subject that you have been learning about at school, or on a subject that especially interests you.
a) Make careful notes about the subject.
b) Draw small versions of the diagrams that you would use to give your talk.
c) Write some brief notes on cards for the talk.
   Perhaps your teacher will choose you to give a talk to the class, or to another class. Good luck!

Fables

Fables are stories which try to teach a lesson.
Most fables have animals as the main characters,
like the second one here.

Common beginning for fables

One character is often poor

Once upon a time a poor
stonecutter was breaking slates at
the foot of an Indian mountain.
Sweat gleamed on his face as he
chip-chipped at the rock face.
He stopped for a rest and sat on a
flat stone. Looking up at the sky,
he saw a big dark cloud, all on
its own, sailing across the blue.
How wonderful it must be to be a
cloud, he thought; to float in the
air far from the backbreaking
drudgery of rock-bashing. Yes, he
thought, I wish I were that cloud.

Often there is magic

Now the rock he happened to be sitting on was a magic one
which had the power to make the wishes of those who sat on it
come true. In the twinkling of an eye, the stonecutter became a
cloud. How splendid it felt! There he was, floating free above the
earth, laughing at the tiny humans scurrying about their work.
Why, he thought, there's the king at the head of a procession of
his nobles. What a stuck-up lot they look! I'll give them a shock.
So he rained on them.

You should have seen the dignified march turn into a
shambles as the magnificently dressed courtiers threw their
cloaks over their heads and ran for cover. The cloud laughed till
his sides ached. He was still laughing when the wind rose, grew
stronger and blew him away from land and out over the sea.

Things look fine, then something awful happens

'Hullo,' he said to himself, 'this isn't so good. I don't like
being blown around like this. I hope the wind dies down soon.'
But it did not; it got worse. Powerful gusts hurled the poor cloud
along at breakneck speed and left him breathless and confused.
He found himself blown right around the world and back to the

mountain. As he looked down on its peaceful bulk, he said to himself, 'How steady that mountain looks! What a quiet, pleasant life it must lead. I do wish I could become that mountain.'

And suddenly he was. What a relief it was to rest in one place. He spent the whole day just daydreaming in the sunshine and loving his new-found peace. Nightfall brought the first snag in his latest life with a sharp frost around his head. The cold made him shiver all night.

Next morning things were better. The rising sun warmed him and he set himself to enjoy a fine day. Suddenly he felt a sharp pain in his side. He winced with the shock. Then came another knife-like dig in the same spot, followed by another. He looked down at the place where he felt the pain. A stonecutter was chip-chipping at his side with a fine edged tool. He looked more closely at the man and – yes! It was himself in human form!

How miserable I feel, thought the mountain. Here I am suffering, while the stonecutter is free of pain. When his work is done, he can go home and live among his loved ones... I do wish I were human again.

Immediately he became a stonecutter once more.

from *101 School Assembly Stories* by Frank Carr

> The stonecutter thinks he has escaped an awful situation

> The stonecutter finds himself in a worse situation

The second fable teaches us that, if you have to give yourself lots of reasons for doing something that will hurt or upset someone else, you probably shouldn't be doing it.

One morning a wolf was drinking at a stream when, looking up, he saw a plump lamb drinking a little way downstream. He moved quietly up behind the little creature and snarled, 'Good morning, breakfast.'

'Are you going to eat me?' asked the terrified lamb.

'Indeed I am,' said the wolf, showing all his pointed teeth in a wicked smile.

'Please don't,' pleaded the lamb. 'After all, I've never done you any harm.'

'Never done me any harm!' exclaimed the wolf. 'What about last winter? What about the day you hid behind the hedge and shouted, "Who's afraid of the big, bad wolf?"'

'But I wasn't even born last winter!' said the lamb. 'You can see that I'm only a few weeks old.'

'It was your brother,' said the wolf. 'He looked exactly like you –

two ears, a fluffy coat, four legs, the lot. Yes, I'm sure it was your brother.'

'But I haven't got a brother… Look, you have no real reason to hurt me. I've never offended you in any way.'

The wolf thought for a moment and then said, 'What about just now?… You had your dirty little snout in my drinking water.'

'You forget,' said the lamb, 'that I was drinking downstream from you. The water around my mouth was flowing away from you, not towards you.'

'Hmm,' said the wolf. 'But I'm going to eat you all the same.'

'Why?' implored the lamb. 'Give me one good reason why you should eat me.'

The wolf thought long and seriously. Then he said, 'I've got it! You wrecked my new home the other day…

'You were running about so much that your paws caused a small earthquake and the bank fell in on my new house.'

'You don't really believe that!' the lamb gasped.

'I certainly do,' said the wolf, and without another word he scoffed down the unfortunate lamb.

adapted from La Fontaine

Think about it

1. What do you think the stonecutter's life was like?
2. What did the stonecutter think it would be like to be a cloud? Was he right?
3. What did the stonecutter think it would be like to be a mountain? Was he right?
4. What lesson do you think this fable is teaching us?
5. Imagine the stonecutter had wished he was a river and then a tree. Rewrite the story to show:
   a) why he wanted to be each of these things
   b) what went wrong.

Now try these

1. Make a list of the excuses that the wolf made for eating the lamb.
2. Do you think the wolf really believed what he was saying?
3. Using the fable you have just read as a model, write a story which shows one of the following:
   a) a person finding excuses for not doing a piece of homework
   b) an animal character finding excuses for stealing another animal's food.

Writing for an audience

When you are writing, you have to be aware of your audience. This means who you are writing for, as readers of your work. This fable has been written for older children.

The Farmer, his Son and the Donkey

Sets the scene

One day a farmer and his son where going to market with their donkey. The donkey plodded on in front while the farmer and his son walked behind.

Shows the farmer doing what the woman suggested

Suddenly, a woman called out to them, 'Why are you both walking? Your son could ride on the donkey.' The farmer told his son to get on the donkey and they went on their way.

Shows the farmer doing what the old men suggested

Further along some old men shouted to them, 'Why is that young, fit boy riding while his father walks? It's disgusting. Young people have no consideration nowadays.' Quickly, the farmer told his son to get down and he climbed on the donkey.

Shows the farmer doing what the two women suggested

They hadn't been going for very long when two old women shouted at them. 'Look at that farmer on the donkey while his poor son trails behind!' Sighing, the farmer told his son to get up behind him and they went on their way.

Shows the farmer doing what the boys suggested

A little further along the road, the farmer and his son encountered a gang of boys. They insulted the farmer and his son, saying they were monsters to make the donkey carry such a heavy burden. 'You should carry the donkey!' they jeered.

The farmer made the donkey lie down and then he tied the animal's feet together. He got a long pole, put it between the donkey's legs and he and his son carried the donkey upside down. As they came to a bridge, the farmer stumbled and fell. The donkey slipped into the river and was drowned.

Tells what the farmer has learnt

The farmer said bitterly, 'From now on I will make my own mind up about what is the right thing to do. You can't please all of the people all of the time!

adapted from Aesop

This is the same story written as a picture book for very young children.

A farmer and his son were
going to market.

A woman said the farmer's son
should ride on the donkey.

Some old men said the farmer
should ride on the donkey.

Two women said they should both
ride on the donkey.

Some boys said that the farmer and
his son should carry the donkey.

The farmer and his son carried the donkey.
The farmer slipped on a bridge and the donkey fell into the river.

The farmer was cross. He said he would
never again listen to what people told him to do.

Think about it

1. Why do you think the first version of the story is suitable for older children but would not be suitable for very young children?
2. Use a dictionary to find the meanings of these words from the story:
   a) consideration b) encountered c) burden
3. What are the differences between the stories written for the two audiences?
4. Why do you think the picture story is more suitable for very young children?

Now try this

Read this fable about the beetle and the eagle.

A hare was in great need of help when chased by an eagle. The only creature in sight at the time was a beetle. The hare begged the beetle for help. The beetle told the hare to have courage and, on seeing the eagle approach, told the bird not to hurt the hare. The eagle laughed at the tiny beetle and ate the hare before its eyes.

The beetle took revenge on the proud eagle. It watched the eagle make its nest, then flew up to the nest and rolled the eagle's eggs out, breaking them. This went on and on, till the eagle took refuge with Zeus, the ruler of the gods. The eagle begged Zeus to provide a safe place for the eggs. Zeus allowed the bird to lay its eggs in his lap.

When the beetle saw this, it made a ball of dung and flew high above Zeus to drop the dung into his lap. Without thinking, Zeus got up to shake off the dung – and tipped out the eggs.

adapted from Aesop

Write the story of the beetle and the eagle as a picture book for a very young child.
Plan and write your work in this order.

a) Understanding the story
   Before you can rewrite the story for a younger child, you must make sure you understand it.
   Look up any words you are not sure of in a dictionary.
   Ask your teacher if there is any part of the story you do not understand.

b) Dividing up the plot
   You need to work out how many pictures you will need to tell the story.
   Work out which part of the story each picture will show and draw the pictures in a sketchy form in pencil.
   You do this because, once you add the words, you may find you have to change some of the pictures. You may also need to add some.

c) Writing
   Once you have pencil drawings, called roughs, write the part of the story that goes with each drawing.
   You will need to make the words very simple.

d) Final draft
   When you have matched the words to the pictures, you need to draw the pictures very carefully and colour them.
   Use one page for each drawing, leaving enough room underneath each picture for the words.
   Write the words neatly or type them on the computer, and you will have your picture book.

e) The cover
   Turn back to Unit 1 and read about book covers again. You could make a book cover for your picture book.

Writing narrative poems

Narrative poems are poems which tell a story. Like a story, they have a setting, characters and plot.

The characters

The setting, lines 1 and 2

The plot, lines 3 to 6

Some lines have a rhyme inside

The Owl and the Pussy-cat

The Owl and the Pussy-cat went to sea
   In a beautiful pea-green boat,
They took some honey, and plenty of money
   Wrapped up in a five-pound note.
The Owl looked up to the stars above,
   And sang to a small Guitar,
'O lovely Pussy! O Pussy, my love,
   What a beautiful Pussy you are,
     You are
     You are!
   What a beautiful Pussy you are!'

A nonsense story

Lines 2 and 4 always rhyme

Lines 6 and 8 always rhyme

Lines 9 and 10 repeat the last two words of line 8

Line 11 is a repeat of line 8

Plot, rest of poem

Pussy said to the Owl, 'You elegant fowl!
    How charmingly sweet you sing!
O let us be married! too long we have tarried:
    But what shall we do for a ring?'
They sailed away, for a year and a day,

A new setting

    To the land where the Bong-tree grows
And there in a wood a Piggy-wig stood
    With a ring at the end of his nose,

Another character

        His nose,
        His nose,
    With a ring at the end of his nose.

'Dear Pig, are you willing to sell for one shilling
    Your ring?' Said the Piggy, 'I will.'
So they took it away, and were married next day
    By the Turkey who lives on the hill.

Another character

They dined on mince, and slices of quince,

New settings

    Which they ate with a runcible spoon;
And hand in hand, on the edge of the sand,
    They danced by the light of the moon,
        The moon,
        The moon,
    They danced by the light of the moon.

Edward Lear

Think about it

1. The story in the poem has four different settings. What are they?
2. The story in the poem has four characters. Who are they?
3. Copy out a line from each verse which has a rhyme inside it.
4. Copy out the rhyming words in verse 2.
5. In your own words, write what you think these words in the poem mean:
   a) elegant
   b) tarried
   c) dined
6. In your own words, write the story of 'The Owl and the Pussy-cat' as a picture book for a young child.

Now try this

Write another verse for the poem showing what the Owl and the Pussy-cat did when they left the 'land where the Bong-tree grows'.

a) Begin by making notes on the following:
   Setting
   Where will the Owl and the Pussy-cat sail to next?
   Characters
   The Owl and the Pussy-cat will be in the next verse but you may need other characters. Who will they meet?
   Plot
   What will happen to them?

b) Make notes on how Edward Lear organised his poem:
   – How many lines in each verse?
   – Which lines always rhyme?
   – Does he always use a rhyme inside a line in each verse?
   – Which lines always repeat the last two words of Line 8?
   – Which line is always repeated at the end of each verse?

c) Write a rough draft of your verse. Don't worry if it doesn't yet rhyme in all the right places.

d) When you have your rough draft, look at the parts you think don't work well. Two ways you can improve these are by changing words that are difficult to rhyme, and by changing the order of words in a line.

e) When you have improved your verse, write it out neatly and illustrate it.

Linking words and phrases

Certain words and phrases are useful to link sentences and thoughts when we write explanations.

When the rains fail

Linking words
and phrases

In many countries food crops will grow throughout the year. **Unfortunately**, however, there are some countries where occasionally the rains fail, **and there is** drought. **When this happens**, the crops wither, **and as a result**, the population may go without food. **If this continues**, people begin to starve and some even die. The animals also die, and the seed that should be saved for planting next year's crop needs to be used right away to keep people alive. **As a result**, even if the rainfall returns the following year, **there may be** no seed to plant **and so** no crops to harvest to feed the people and their animals.

Here are the notes that were made before writing the article above.

some countries rain frequent, others occasional;
drought; crops die; hunger for people + animals;
problem if use seed = more hunger next year

Some of the useful linking words and phrases are printed in bold letters in this account. You can see how they help the writer explain the problem.

Think about it

Here are some notes about farming in countries without serious rainfall shortages, but where other problems may occur. Write a sentence from each set of notes. The first has been done to help you.

a) winter; very wet; heavy soil; difficult to get tractor on field; difficult to plough

As a result of the very wet winter, the soil had been left very heavy and the farmer found it difficult to get his tractor onto the fields to plough.

b) warm spring; early blossom; late frost; wrecked apple crop
c) planted extra potatoes; very good crop; too many potatoes in shops; price to farmers very low
d) good crop; start harvesting; machine breaks down; mended; then rains

Now try these

1. When writing explanations or reports, it is better not to write in the first person, which means using personal words like *I*, *me*, *we*, *you*.
   Here is part of an account written by a pupil when his class made a visit to an agricultural museum.
   Rewrite the passage in the third person, using pronouns like *he*, *she*, *they*, *it*. The first sentence has been done to help you.

   I found the museum interesting. We travelled a long way to get there but we all thought it was worth the effort.

   The museum was interesting. It was a long journey, but it was worth the effort.

   The things that we all liked most were the animals. I found the shire horses especially interesting, but I also liked the breeds of sheep and cattle that are now rare. We also saw many old-fashioned machines, including the early steam-driven traction engines. I was surprised how many people used to live in the villages. We could work this out by looking at old pictures of harvest time, when you could see lots of labourers working in the fields, cutting and collecting the crops.

2. Choose a book about farming or another subject you are working on. Make brief notes from one chapter or section, close the book and write the information in your own words, using interesting linking words and phrases.

3. Write an explanation and give your reasons for what should be done by people from rich countries like Britain for the people in very poor countries. Try not to use the word 'I' in your account.

Clear and concise explanations

Whether writing about facts or expressing opinions, try to make your writing clear and concise.

Living in different communities

Brief introduction to the subject

Living in any community has its good and its bad points.

Very often people can think of what is wrong with where they live, and wish they lived somewhere else, such as places they see when they are on holiday.

Living in a small, country community has advantages and disadvantages. Here are a few of each.

Clear and concise descriptions

Advantages:
It is possible to know everybody.
There is plenty of open space.
The air is fresh and unpolluted.
There is much less traffic than in towns.
Most people feel safer in villages, where there is less crime.
The houses and cottages are pretty.

Disadvantages:
It is difficult to keep yourself to yourself.
It can be a long way to the nearest town.
It is necessary to travel to the nearest town for schools, shops, doctors, etc.
There aren't many buses or trains in villages.
There isn't much work for grown-ups.
There are fewer entertainments.

Think about it

1. Would you prefer to live in a village or in the town? Write a short account giving your main reasons. Use these phrases to begin each paragraph.

   If I could choose, I would prefer to live in ...

   There are several reasons for this. The main one is that ...

   Another reason is ...

   I also think that ...

   From what I have written you can understand why ...

2. Using question 1 as a model, write about the main disadvantages of living where you live at the moment.

Now try these

1. Look carefully at the pictures. Make a list of the main advantages and disadvantages of living in any two of them.
2. If you could choose anywhere in the world to live, where would it be? Give your reasons in a clear and concise way. Don't forget to mention any disadvantages.

Using information

When researching facts for a report, keep a note of where you found the information. Then make sure you tell your readers which books you have used.

Magnets: from rocks to computers

Source of definition

The word 'magnet', according to *The Concise Oxford Dictionary*, comes from the Greek word 'magnesetos', which means stone of Magnesia.

Most of us assume magnets are made in factories. They are now, but the original magnets were certainly not made in a factory or bought from a shop. As Nigel Bennett explains:

Writer of the book where information was found

'The magnet has a very long history and can be traced back to a part of the country of Greece called Thessaly. Many thousands of years ago, in a district called Magnesia, people discovered a rock which seemed to do strange things.

'The rock, called magnetite, was found to attract anything made of iron. It also had other properties. It was later found to rotate in a certain direction and point north or south.'

It is surprising how much we use magnets in modern technology. Magnets are found in everything from video cassettes to computers. In his book, *Electricity and Magnetism*, Dr Brian Knapp tells us that:

Title and author of another source of information

'Magnets don't have to look like bars. Some of the most useful are shaped into tapes and disks.

'A cassette tape is a long plastic ribbon, coated with minute iron particles (look for the non-shiny side). As the tape moves

it goes past a tiny electromagnet called a recording head. Electric signals reaching the recording head set up patterns of magnetism on the tape.

'Computers store information on disks that look something like a record. The disk, often called a floppy disk because it is made of bendy plastic, has an iron coating on its surface.

'The computer "reads" from and "writes" onto the disk using a small head just like the tape recorder. The disk shown here has 800 000 pieces of information stored on it in magnetic form. The biggest disks can store many millions of pieces of information.'

Bibliography

1 Bennett, Nigel, *Magnets, Batteries and Globes*, Macmillan
2 Knapp, Brian, *Electricity and Magnetism*, Atlantic Europe Publishing Company

More details of the books mentioned

Think about it

Write a sentence to answer each of these questions.
a) Who wrote about the history of magnets in his book?
b) What was the book called?
c) Who published the book?
d) Which dictionary is quoted in the passage?
e) Write the names of two other dictionaries.
f) Whose book tells about the use of magnets in computers?
g) What was the book called?
h) Who published the book?
i) What other sort of book could you refer to for information about magnets?
j) Make a list of the author, title and publisher of three other books in which you can find useful information on magnets and magnetism.

Now try these

1. Write a few paragraphs about other uses of magnets or write about the discovery and uses of electricity. Use the books in your school library or from home. Don't forget to use quotations from the authors of the books you use (put these inside speech marks), and write the details of their books in a bibliography at the end of your work.
2. Choose a subject that you are learning about at the moment. Make a list of books in your library in which you might find information about the subject. Make a bibliography. Use the surnames of the authors and list the books in alphabetical order by authors' names.

UNIT 16

Writing from a character's point of view

To help you understand how a character may be feeling, it is useful to 'put yourself in their shoes.'

A state in America

A young slave girl

Night music droned through the slave quarters of Jeb Hensen's Virginia plantation. The words couldn't be heard but they were there beneath the rise and fall of the melody.

Julilly hummed them as she sat in the doorway of her cabin, waiting for Mammy Sally to come home from cooking in the Big House kitchen. She was as still and as black as the night. The words of the song beat in her head.

> When Israel was in Egypt's land
> Let my people go
> Oppressed so hard, they could not stand
> Let my people go.

Master

The slaves are worried

Old Massa Hensen didn't like the song. He said it came when there were whisperings and trouble around. There were whisperings tonight. They murmured beneath the chirping of the crickets. They crept from ear to ear as soundless as the flickering of the fireflies...

Because it reminded the singers they are slaves

The whisperings that hung in the night-time air had started this morning when Old John, the coachman, drove Missy Hensen into town. Julilly and the other slaves heard about it later.

Mrs Hensen

Missy Hensen sat uneasily and restless in the carriage seat. She talked to Old John of moving North and of selling things. She talked of how her husband, Jeb Hensen, was old and sick and had to go to the hospital in Richmond. She said they had no kin to leave things to...

When Missy Hensen and Old John drove into town, there was excitement on the Court House lawn. Missy Hensen pretended not to see. Old John, who couldn't read, heard the white folks speak of handbills plastered on the Court House door: "WILL PAY TOP PRICES TOMORROW FOR PRIME FIELD HANDS," they read.

He realises what may happen to them

Old John's hands trembled on the horses' reins. A slave trader from the deep South was coming to their town to buy tomorrow! Jeb Hensen was making plans to move!

The southernmost states of America

Old John and the other slaves at the Hensen plantation knew about the buying of Virginia slaves. Word of it spread like a wind-whipped flame from one plantation to another. Rumours spread. Some said the buyer

These rumours will make the slaves frightened

lined the slaves up one by one like cows and pigs. They'd sell a mother to one man and her children to another.

'In the deep South,' folks said, 'even the little children tote hoes bigger than themselves, to chop the cotton. Then they get whipped 'cause they don't finish the work the overseer set out for them.'

Massa Hensen treats his slaves reasonably well

Massa Hensen didn't whip much on his plantation.

'Too soft-hearted,' some of the slave owners said.

From *Underground to Canada* by Barbara Smucker

Think about it

1. The opening of this story makes you want to go on reading to find out what happens.
   Write a list of questions that you hope will be answered by the author in the rest of the story.
2. The title of this book is *Underground to Canada*. What do you think some of the slaves try to do?

Now try this

Imagine you are Julilly, the young slave girl.
You have heard the rumours about Massa Hensen selling the plantation.
You know that a slave trader from the deep South is coming to buy slaves.
You know how slaves are treated in the deep South.
Write your thoughts and feelings.

Dialogue

Dialogue is important in stories because it often helps us to get to know a character and it also carries the story along.

Jazeera sipped her drink and turned her attention to a severe-looking woman who had just entered the shop. She was followed by three trailing daughters of various ages, all looking bored. The woman, who was obviously their mother, began choosing sets of bangles for each of her daughters, without once consulting them as to which colour they would prefer. The girls for their part stood in a disgruntled line and stared at Jazeera...

Jazeera turned to Ibrahim to avoid meeting the row of silent eyes. He was arguing with their mother.

'But you must give me a better price than that.'

'Twenty rupees each.'

'But I'm buying six sets. I will give you a hundred rupees and no more.'

'Done!'

Ibrahim held out his hand for the crinkled note.

'You would not get bangles of this quality, for that price anywhere else, madame,' he smiled.

The woman snorted and ushered her reluctant brood back out into the busy street...

Jazeera was confused. If the bangles were twenty rupees each, then six sets should have cost 120 rupees. That meant that Ibrahim had sold them too cheaply. He was cheating her uncle!

> **The lady and Ibrahim 'haggle' about the price**

> **Type of money used in India**

> **Jazeera does not understand bargaining**

Just then Uncle Salim returned. Before Jazeera had a chance to say anything, Ibrahim thrust the 100 rupee note into his hand.

'Six sets. I just sold six sets for a hundred rupees!' Ibrahim's eyes danced with glee.

Ibrahim is obviously pleased with himself

'Very good,' Uncle congratulated him.

Jazeera couldn't stay quiet. 'Uncle,' she said softly. 'They should have been twenty rupees each.'

She is not sure he got a good price

Uncle Salim looked at her worried face and crouched down beside her. 'Let me explain,' he said. 'Shopping here is not like shopping in England, where everything has a fixed price on the label. In India we argue about the price. The shopkeeper will start by saying a price much higher than he expects to get. Then the customer says a price much lower than he or she expects to pay. Slowly the shopkeeper lowers his price and the customer raises his until they both agree, somewhere in the middle.'

Uncle Salim is explaining what happens to Jazeera and also to the reader

Jazeera frowned. 'That all sounds very complicated.'

'Yes,' laughed Uncle. 'But so much more fun than shopping in England. Ibrahim here is a very good salesman. One hundred rupees is much more than I would have sold the bangles for.' Uncle slapped Ibrahim playfully, on the back. 'I know that my shop is in good hands when I leave it with him...'

From *Jazeera in the Sun* by Lisa Bruce

Think about it

1. Explain in your own words what you think these phrases mean.
   a) in a disgruntled line
   b) her reluctant brood
   c) very complicated
2. The method of shopping in the story is called 'bartering', whereas in England most things are a 'fixed price'.
   Which kind of shopping do you prefer? Give your reasons.

Now try this

Uncle Salim has explained to Jazeera the difference between shopping in England and shopping in India.

Imagine another woman now comes into the shop and wants to buy a necklace. She is willing to pay 50 rupees. Jazeera wants to be a 'good salesman' like Ibrahim.

Write the conversation between Jazeera and the customer.

Writing about books

When you have read a story, you probably think 'That was good' or 'I didn't like that'. Here is a way of keeping a record of the books you read, and of writing in more detail about them.

This part of a reading record gives information about the book.

Title _Journey to Jo'burg_

Author _Beverley Naidoo_

Published by _Collins_

Setting

The story takes place in

> South Africa

Characters

The main characters are

> Naledi – a thirteen-year-old girl
> Tiro - her brother who is nine
> Dineo – their baby sister

Plot

The story is about

> Naledi and Tiro walk 300 miles to Johannesburg to find their mother because their baby sister is ill.

Think about it

1. Where do you find the title and author of a book?
2. Where might you find who published the book?
3. Make a chart like the one above for the story you have just finished reading.
4. What other information about the book could you put on this reading record?

This is a useful part of a reading record because it gives your opinion.

Some of the ideas in the story

> 1. How awful it must be to live so far away from your mother.
> 2. How brave even young children can be.
> 3. How unfairly black people are treated in South Africa.

Think about what the story is trying to tell you

The episode I liked best

> When the children tried to get on a 'whites only' bus and were helped by Grace Mbatha.

Your opinion

Why I liked this episode best

> I felt very sorry for the children when they couldn't get on the bus, but very pleased when Grace helped them to find their mother.

Reasons I would or would not like my friends to read this book

> I would like my friends to read this book because it shows how difficult life is for children in a different part of the world, and how people can succeed even when everything seems to be against them.

Now try these

1. The part of the reading record needing your opinion makes you think carefully about a book. Add it to the first part of the chart you made for the story you have just read and complete it.
2. Look at the two parts of the chart. What is the difference between the kind of information you write in the first part of the chart and the kind of information you write in the second part?

Letters to persuade

Letters written to persuade someone should gain attention, be sensible, and argue your points strongly.

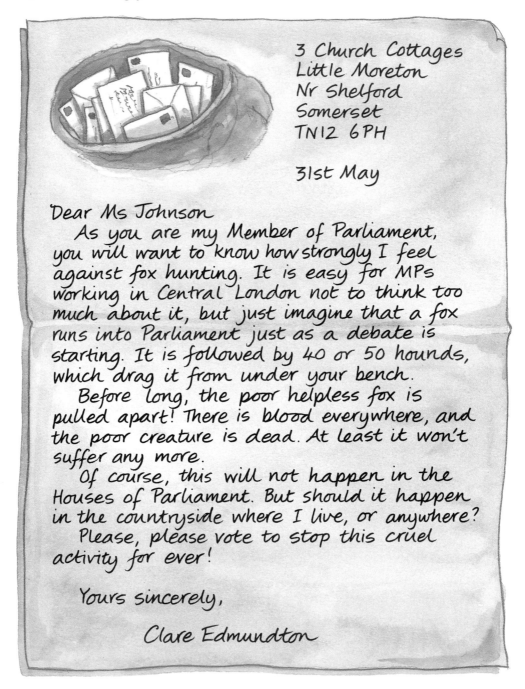

3 Church Cottages
Little Moreton
Nr Shelford
Somerset
TN12 6PH

31st May

Dear Ms Johnson

As you are my Member of Parliament, you will want to know how strongly I feel against fox hunting. It is easy for MPs working in Central London not to think too much about it, but just imagine that a fox runs into Parliament just as a debate is starting. It is followed by 40 or 50 hounds, which drag it from under your bench.

Before long, the poor helpless fox is pulled apart! There is blood everywhere, and the poor creature is dead. At least it won't suffer any more.

Of course, this will not happen in the Houses of Parliament. But should it happen in the countryside where I live, or anywhere?

Please, please vote to stop this cruel activity for ever!

Yours sincerely,

Clare Edmundton

Think about it

1. Make a chart listing all the reasons for and against fox hunting. Clare's letter gives you some of the reasons for banning it. Can you think of others? There are also people who write to their MP saying fox hunting should be allowed to continue. Make a list of the reasons that they might give.

2. When you are arguing your side, it helps to be able to think of what people with the opposite view might say. Write a letter as if you believe fox hunting is a good thing and should be allowed to continue, even if you oppose it.

Now try these

1. There are many other issues that people feel strongly about. Very often there are two opposite points of view on these issues. Choose something that is important in your town or village, such as a new road that some people want and others don't, or a new supermarket that some people want and others don't. Write a list of the reasons for and against.

   If you can't think of a big issue in your area, choose something else that is important to you, such as whether live cattle should be exported, or whether whale hunting should be allowed, or whether large creatures should be kept in cages in zoos. Then write a list of the reasons for and against one of these things.

2. Once you have clearly sorted out the arguments, you are ready to write a real letter, either to your Member of Parliament **or** to your local councillor **or** to the manager of the zoo. Draft it first, then edit it.

   Finally, when you are happy with your letter, write it **or** type it on a computer, and send it off!

Behind the news

Newspapers tell us the news, but they also give the opinions of their owners and editors. Usually these opinions are in the editorial. Here are a story and an editorial on the same event.

Name of newspaper

WALLINGTON STANDARD

Monday 3 Ma

Date of this edition

Headline

HUNDREDS MARCH ON TOWN HALL

Reporter's name

Factual report of what took place

Hilary Frost reports

The police closed the roads around the centre of the town on Friday evening as hundreds of people, young and old alike, converged on the Town Hall. The demonstration was timed to coincide with a meeting of the Council to discuss the future of Fryer Street Swimming Pool. The pool, which has now been closed for nearly six months, is in desperate need of refurbishment. The final straw came when the heating system failed, and the pool could no longer be used.

The demonstration was peaceful, though noisy. A police spokeswoman said she could not remember such a big protest demonstration in the town. She estimated that nearly a thousand people marched from the main car park, carrying banners and shouting protests. The protests reached a peak when news leaked from the meeting inside the Council Chamber that no decision had been reached, and the matter would be discussed again at next month's meeting.

Mrs Heather Painter, chairperson of the Residents' Association, addressed the crowd, and to loud cheers promised that the fight to save the pool would go on.

WHO'S MAKING THE DECISIONS?

Editorials have few facts, but lots of opinions

Our front page reports on the campaign to save our swimming pool.

Surely it is time for our councillors to see sense. For too long they have been sitting on their hands over the closure of the swimming pool, not wanting to accept responsibility for either closing it, or for the raising of taxes to keep it open.

We vote for these people to take responsibility and to take decisions – not to run away from them.

It has also come to our attention that there might be some dirty dealing behind the scenes. Two of our councillors, whom we can't yet name for legal reasons, may have an interest in a new housing development that would be built on the site of the pool if it is closed.

This is not good enough. We expect the highest standards from those in public office in our town. As it is we have too many who want the glory but don't have the backbone to make a decision or, worse, might be trying to line their own pockets at the expense of future generations of young families who would enjoy the recreational facilities of a town swimming pool.

Think about it

1. Look again at the front page story. Answer these questions about the facts of the story.
   a) Why were people demonstrating?
   b) How many people marched?
   c) Why did they decide to march on Friday evening?
   d) How long had the swimming pool been closed?
   e) Why was it closed?
   f) Where did the march begin?
   g) Was a decision about the future of the pool made at the Council meeting?
   h) Who is chairperson of the Residents' Association?

2. How many of the facts in question 1 could you have answered just from reading the editorial?

Now try these

1. Look at the editorial again. Write these sentences and phrases in another way.
   a) It is time for our councillors to see sense.
   b) For too long they have been sitting on their hands.
   c) We vote for these people to take responsibility and to take decisions – not to run away from them.
   d) some dirty dealing behind the scenes
   e) want the glory
   f) don't have the backbone to make a decision
   g) line their own pockets

2. The editorial writer uses some words, like 'surely' and 'we vote for', to persuade us that he or she is on our side. Write out any other words and phrases that are like this.

3. Think of something that has happened recently at school or in your local area. Write a factual account about it for your local paper or school magazine, then write an editorial giving your opinion.

Preparing an argument

Before talking to a group of people, it is important to plan your arguments and to think about all the points of view.

Bernadette is preparing to talk to the class about whether animals should be kept in zoos.

First she makes two lists, with brief notes of arguments **in favour of** zoos and arguments **against** zoos.

Arguments for:	Arguments against:
• Without zoos we wouldn't be able to see most animals in real life.	• Zoo cages are like animal prisons.
• Animals are well looked after and have enough food.	• Zoos are unnatural.
• Animals are never hunted in zoos.	• Animals are happier in the wild.
• Sick animals are seen by a vet.	• The more animals captured for zoos, the fewer left in the wild.
• Rare animals are protected.	• Capturing and transporting animals to zoos can be cruel.
• Scientists can study animals more easily in zoos.	• Why should animals be stared at by humans? We wouldn't like it!

Next she thinks carefully about which arguments are the most important to her and summarises her conclusion based on these.

My conclusion, having thought about all the arguments, is that zoos should be allowed, but animals should always be in large open shelters. Animals should be bred from other animals already in zoos, and hardly ever captured from the wild.

Now Bernadette is ready to give her talk to the class.

After her talk, Bernadette's teacher asked her to write about her viewpoint on zoos for the school magazine. This is what she wrote on her computer.

Our class has been discussing whether animals should be kept in zoos. Nearly all of us have enjoyed a day at the zoo, but we are now thinking about whether zoos are good places for animals to be kept.

Some of the good things about zoos are that animals are usually well looked after and have enough food and water. They are never hunted, sick animals can be seen by a vet and rare animals that might die out in the wild are bred and protected. Also, zoos are good places for scientists to study animals. Without zoos we wouldn't be able to see animals from all over the world in real life.

However, we also think that zoo cages are like animal prisons, and we wouldn't want to be kept in a cage all day. Zoos are unnatural and animals are happier in the wild. We also think that the more animals are captured for zoos, the fewer are left in the wild. Some of our class also wonder why animals should be stared at by humans. After all, we wouldn't like it!

Our conclusion, having thought about all the arguments, is that zoos should be allowed, but animals should always be in large open shelters with lots of room for exercise, and they should be bred from other animals already in zoos, and hardly ever captured from the wild.

Think about it

1. Which of Bernadette's arguments in favour of zoos are you most persuaded by? Give your reasons.
2. Which of Bernadette's arguments against zoos are you most persuaded by? Give your reasons.
3. Give another reason of your own in favour of keeping animals in zoos. Give another reason against.
4. Do you agree with Bernadette's conclusion? Give your reasons for the way you feel.

Now try these

1. Write out a chart and notes for giving a talk to your class on one of these topics. If you prefer you can choose a topic of your own.

   • Smoking should be totally banned.
   • School uniforms are a good thing.
   • Ball games should not be allowed in playgrounds.
   • The government should set a minimum level for pocket money.

2. Write an article for the school magazine from your notes, using Bernadette's as a model.

Leaflets

Leaflets are produced to tell us something, or to persude us about something.

Strong title/heading

Punchy catch phrase

Concise presentation of the main message

More detail clearly set out using bullet points

Short, sharp conclusion

FIREWORK FUN

Guy Fawkes says:

Keep safe! Have fun!

Every year hundreds of people are badly burnt on Guy Fawkes Day. Make sure it's not your turn this year!

Follow the firework code:

- Keep fireworks in a closed box.
- Take fireworks out one at a time and close the box each time.
- Read the instructions on each firework by the light of a torch.
- Light all fireworks at arm's length.
- Never return to a firework once it is lit.
- Never throw fireworks.
- Never put fireworks in your pocket.
- Keep all pets indoors.

Best of all, let someone else do the work, while you just watch and wonder. Enjoy bigger, better firework fun at a public display.

Beware!

Fireworks are dangerous, so keep away from them if you don't want to be hurt. The firework manufacturers have worked out a set of rules which should be followed by everyone.

The eight rules say: keep fireworks in a closed box; take fireworks out one at a time and close the box each time; read the instructions on each firework by the light of a torch; light all fireworks at arm's length; never return to a firework once it is lit; never throw fireworks; never put fireworks in your pocket; and keep all pets indoors.

Think about this and you'll agree it would be far better if you don't have your own fireworks, but instead go to a public firework display.

Think about it

1. Write a sentence to answer each question.
   a) Why should fireworks be kept in a closed box?
   b) Why should you never return to a firework that looks as though it has gone out?
   c) What is wrong with keeping fireworks in your pocket?
   d) Why don't pets enjoy fireworks?
2. Which of these two leaflets would you be more likely to read? Give your reasons.
3. Eight rules are a lot for people to think about at one time. Choose one of the rules and make a small poster which will really persuade people that it is a sensible rule to follow. Think how you can make your poster really eye-catching.
4. These rules are set out on small one-page leaflets. Imagine that you have been asked to write and design a four-page leaflet about the firework code. Fold a fairly large piece of paper in half. Think what will go on each page. The front page should strongly capture interest, and make the reader want to read on.

Now try these

1. Leaflets are useful in trying to persuade other people. Choose one of these ideas, or think of one yourself, as a subject for a leaflet.

   • Old, retired people should not have to pay for television licences.
   • Cycle helmets should be compulsory.
   • Bulls should never be kept in fields which have public footpaths.
   • Children under twelve should never be given homework.

   First make some notes of what you want to say. Make a list of your reasons for what you think.
   Then write it in a concise and persuasive style, thinking carefully about the people who you want to read it.
   Finally design and illustrate your leaflet. If you can, try to design it on a computer.

2. Leaflets are also frequently used to persuade people to buy something. Write and design a leaflet that tries to make us think we should all be eating a new brand of breakfast cereal. (Think of a good name for it!)